13 Colonies

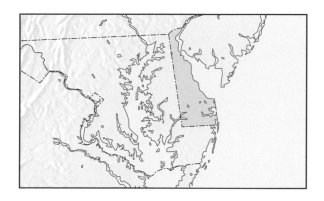

Delaware

13 Colonies

DELAWARE

THE HISTORY OF DELAWARE COLONY, 1638–1776

ROBERTA WIENER AND JAMES R. ARNOLD

Raintree

Chicago, Illinois

© 2005 Raintree
Published by Raintree,
A division of Reed Elsevier, Inc.
Chicago, IL

For information, address the publisher:
Raintree, 100 N. LaSalle, Suite 1200, Chicago, IL 60602

Printed and bound in China

08 07 06 05 04
10 9 8 7 6 5 4 3 2 1

Library of Congress Cataloging-in-Publication Data
Wiener, Roberta, 1952-
   Delaware / Roberta Wiener and James R. Arnold.
      p. cm. -- (13 colonies)
Summary: A detailed look at the formation of the colony of Delaware, its government, and its overall history, plus a prologue on world events in 1638 and an epilogue on Delaware today.
Includes bibliographical references and index.
   ISBN 0-7398-6878-0 (lib. bdg.) -- ISBN 1-4109-0302-8 (pbk.)
   1. Delaware--History--Colonial period, ca. 1600-1775--Juvenile literature. 2. Delaware--History--Revolution, 1775-1783--Juvenile literature. [1. Delaware--History--Colonial period, ca. 1600-1775. 2. Delaware--History--Revolution, 1775-1783.] I. Arnold, James R. II. Title. III. Series: Wiener, Roberta, 1952-   13 colonies.
   F167W495 2004
   975.1'02--DC21

                              2003011056

Title page picture: The Old Swedes Church in Wilmington was built in 1698. It is one of the oldest standing churches in the United States. It started as a Swedish Lutheran church, then became Anglican, and is now Episcopalian.

Opposite: Governor Printz sent men out from the main fort to live in what he called strong houses, because they were solidly built and possible to defend.

The authors wish to thank Walter Kossmann, whose knowledge, patience, and ability to ask all the right questions have made this a better series.

Some words are shown in bold, **like this.** You can find out what they mean by looking in the glossary.

Picture Acknowledgments

Architect of the Capitol: 9 Abby Aldrich Rockefeller Folk Art Museum, Colonial Williamsburg Foundation: 54 Colonial Williamsburg Foundation: 8, 11, 14 inset, 32, 33, 34 U.S. Government Printing Office: 48-49 Hagley Museum & Library, Wilmington, DE: 58 top J.G. Heck, *Iconographic Encyclopedia of Science, Literature, and Art*, 1851: 34-35 Courtesy of the Historical Society of Delaware: Title page, 14, 18, 22, 23 top, 29, 36 bottom, 37, 58 bottom Courtesy of the Historical Society of Delaware and the Colonial Dames of Delaware: 5, 15, 20 bottom, 23 bottom, 28, 39, 44-45 Independence National Historical Park: 35, 50, 51 Eric Inglefield: 57 Library Company of Philadelphia: 13 bottom Library of Congress: 12 top, 13 top, 20 top, 27, 30, 31, 36 top, 38, 40, 41, 43, 46-47, 52 bottom, 53, 59 National Archives: 12 bottom, 21, 46 top, 52 top National Park Service, Colonial National Historical Park: Cover, 16, 17, 24-25, 46 bottom U.S. Naval Historical Center, Washington, DC: 55 U.S. Senate Collection: 6

Contents

PROLOGUE: THE WORLD IN 1638

In the spring of 1638, Sweden began its first permanent colony on the banks of the Delaware River. The Swedish settlement was small in comparison to its neighbors. At this time English colonists already lived in Virginia and Maryland to the south, and in New England to the north. The Dutch had established a colony just to the north, which they called New Netherland. France and Spain also had colonies in North America.

The first European explorers to set foot in North America were the **Vikings**, who came from the same part of Europe as the Swedes. They visited a site on the coast of modern-day Canada before the year 1000. The Vikings beat the other Europeans to America by almost 500 years, but they did not stay there for long. By the time Europeans again began to explore the wider world, the Vikings' explorations had faded from memory.

VIKINGS: SCANDINAVIAN PEOPLE WHO TRAVELED IN LONG-OARED BOATS TO RAID THE EUROPEAN SETTLEMENTS DURING THE 8TH, 9TH, AND 10TH CENTURIES

According to popular legend, the Norwegian Viking, Leif Erikson, was the first European ever to set foot in America. He was one of the first, but probably not the very first. An Icelandic expedition may have beaten him there by more than ten years.

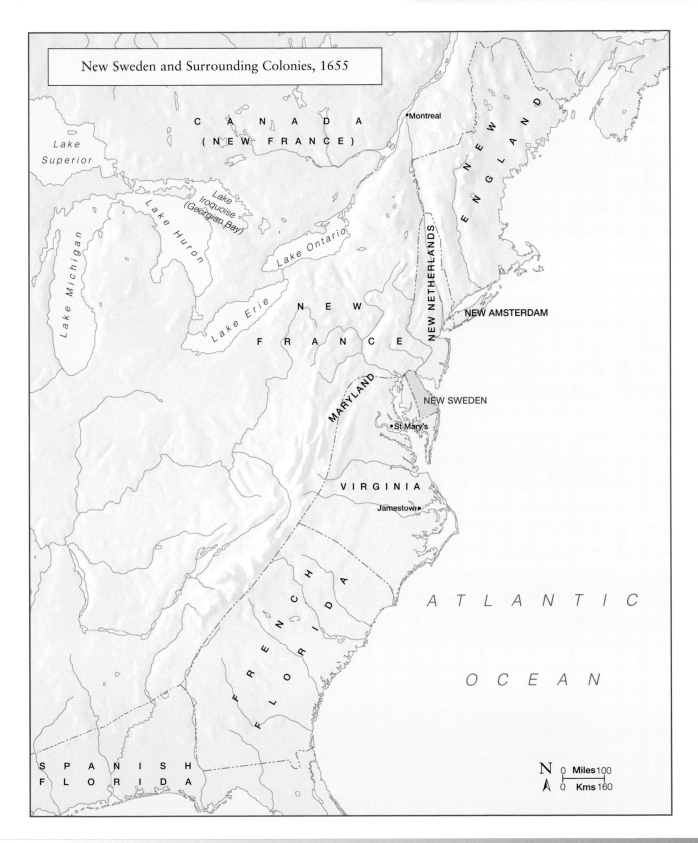

New Sweden and Surrounding Colonies, 1655

Lake Superior

C A N A D A
(N E W   F R A N C E)

•Montreal

N E W   E N G L A N D

Lake Michigan

Lake Huron

Lake Iroquoise (Georgian Bay)

Lake Ontario

Lake Erie

N E W
F R A N C E

NEW NETHERLANDS

NEW AMSTERDAM

MARYLAND

NEW SWEDEN

•St Mary's

V I R G I N I A

Jamestown•

A T L A N T I C

F R E N C H   F L O R I D A

O C E A N

S P A N I S H
F L O R I D A

N

0   Miles 100
0   Kms 160

During the Renaissance, a 150-year period of invention and discovery in Europe, advances in navigation and the building of better sailing ships allowed longer voyages. A new age of exploration dawned, with great seamen from Portugal, Spain, Italy, France, and England sailing into uncharted waters. Beginning in the 1400s, they reached Africa, India, the Pacific Ocean, China, Japan, and Australia. They encountered kingdoms and civilizations that had existed for centuries.

The voyages from Europe to these distant shores were long and dangerous. Explorers had to sail from Europe all the way around Africa. So, European explorers began to sail westward in search of shortcuts. On one such voyage,

A map shows the European view of the world around 1570.

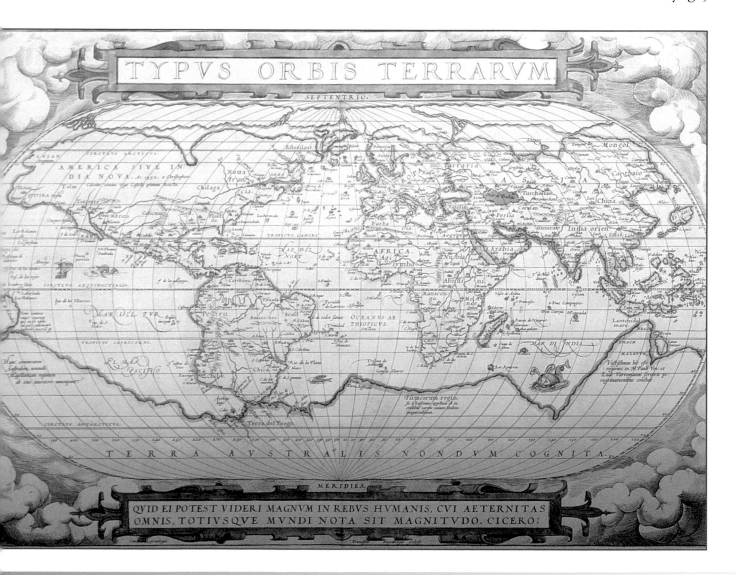

in 1492, Christopher Columbus landed on an island on the far side of the Atlantic Ocean and claimed it for Spain. He thought that he had actually sailed clear around the world and come to an island near India. Years of exploration by numerous sailors would pass before the people of Europe realized that Columbus had been the first European of their era to set foot in a land unknown to them. They called this forgotten land the **New World**, although it was not new to the people who lived there.

After Columbus, Amerigo Vespucci claimed to have reached the New World. Whether he actually did or not, in 1507 a mapmaker put his name on a map, and the New World became **America**, or the Americas. Still look-ing for that shortcut to the riches of Asia, explorers from Portugal, Spain, France, and England continued to sail to North and South America. They began to claim large pieces of these lands for their own nations.

The Spanish were far ahead of other Europeans in the com-petition for land in the Americas, claiming huge portions of both North and South America. They had conquered two mighty Native American empires. The Spanish had introduced the first domestic cattle and horses to the Americas. They had brought European civilization as well, including printing presses and universities.

Yet there remained many places in this newly explored land where no Europeans had yet settled. All of Europe saw America, not just as a possible shortcut to somewhere else, but as a huge empty land with riches waiting to be taken. They also saw America as a new base from which to fight wars with one another.

The Italian navigator Amerigo Vespucci was born in Florence in 1454. Historians believe that he and Columbus had met one another while Vespucci was working for a business that outfitted sailing ships. Vespucci made at least two voyages to the Americas between 1499 and 1502.

I.
SWEDEN AND FRIENDS

The **Dutch** and the Swedes were allies in a long European war of Protestant powers against Catholic powers, one of which was Spain. Known to history as the **Thirty Years' War**, the fighting lasted from 1618 to 1648. During this time, the Dutch fought for their independence from Spain, with the help of Sweden's remarkably strong army.

The **Netherlands** had wanted a **colony** in America, mainly as a base for raiding Spain's American colonies. In 1609 the Dutch hired the English explorer Henry Hudson. Hudson sailed up the Delaware Bay and what would later be named the Hudson River. In 1624 the Netherlands founded a colony, New Netherland, in the region Hudson had explored. The Dutch claimed that New Netherland, centered in present-day New York, included the land now occupied by New Jersey and Delaware.

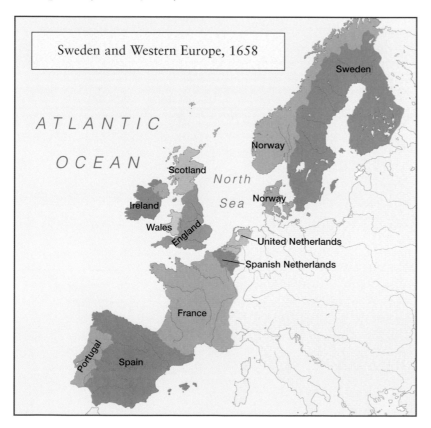

Sweden and Western Europe, 1658

ATLANTIC OCEAN

Sweden
Norway
Scotland
North Sea
Norway
Ireland
Wales
England
United Netherlands
Spanish Netherlands
France
Portugal
Spain

DUTCH: NATIONALITY OF PEOPLE BORN IN HOLLAND OR THE NETHERLANDS

THIRTY YEARS' WAR: A WAR FOUGHT THROUGHOUT EUROPE FROM 1618 TO 1648. THE WAR BEGAN AS A RELIGIOUS WAR BETWEEN ROMAN CATHOLICS AND PROTESTANTS FOR CONTROL OF GERMANY, BUT OTHER NATIONS JOINED THE FIGHTING. ENORMOUS DESTRUCTION OF LIVES AND PROPERTY OCCURRED ACROSS EUROPE.

NETHERLANDS: EUROPEAN NATION FORMED BY THE UNION OF SEVERAL LOW-LYING PROVINCES, INCLUDING HOLLAND. AMSTERDAM IS THE CAPITAL. PEOPLE THERE ARE KNOWN AS "DUTCH."

COLONY: LAND OWNED AND CONTROLLED BY A DISTANT NATION; A COLONIST IS A PERMANENT SETTLER OF A COLONY

OUTPOST: FORT OR SETTLEMENT LOCATED FAR FROM THE MAIN SETTLEMENT

NATIVE AMERICANS: PEOPLE WHO HAD BEEN LIVING IN AMERICA FOR THOUSANDS OF YEARS AT THE TIME THAT THE FIRST EUROPEANS ARRIVED

A group of Dutch merchants disagreed with their government's emphasis on using the colony just as a military **outpost** for fighting Spain. They wanted to form a permanent settlement and develop trade with the **Native Americans** and the English colonists. So they suggested a joint colonization and trading venture to the king of Sweden. King Gustavus Adolphus granted the merchants a **charter** to form a company. However, he died in battle in 1632, and his daughter Christina became the queen of Sweden. She was only six years old at the time, so a group of officials ran Sweden's government. One of Queen Christina's ministers formed the New Sweden Company in 1637. Its stockholders included Dutch merchants and Swedish government officials.

Sweden wanted to make money from fur trading in America. But as a **Lutheran** country, Sweden also believed that Spain, a Catholic country, was getting too powerful. So they too wanted their colony to serve also as a base from which to attack Spain's American colonies. They aimed to settle south of the Dutch colony's main base at New Amsterdam, present-day New York City, and north of England's colony in Maryland. The Dutch merchants, as partners in the New Sweden Company, invested in the New Sweden colony, paying for crewmen and provisions for the first voyages.

Peter Minuit, a French Huguenot (Protestant), had served with the Dutch in New Netherland, and had made the legendary **Manhattan Purchase** for $24 worth of beads. He capably governed the colony of New Netherland between 1626 and 1632, but he made a lot of enemies, and his enemies had him replaced. The Swedes recognized his talents, however, and put him in charge of founding New Sweden.

A merchant's office in the Netherlands in the 17th century

CHARTER: DOCUMENT CONTAINING THE RULES FOR RUNNING AN ORGANIZATION

MANHATTAN PURCHASE: 1626 DUTCH PURCHASE OF MANHATTAN ISLAND, THE CENTER OF PRESENT-DAY NEW YORK CITY, FROM THE LOCAL NATIVE AMERICANS FOR ABOUT $24 WORTH OF TRINKETS AND JEWELRY

2.
ACROSS THE OCEAN

The New Sweden Company outfitted two small vessels for the ocean crossing to the Delaware River valley, the *Kalmar Nyckel* (*Key of Kalmar*) and the *Vogel Grip* (*Griffin*). About half the ships' crewmen were Dutch. Twenty-three Swedish soldiers, equipped with muskets and gunpowder, were assigned to protect the first expedition to settle New Sweden. Few records exist about who was in the first expedition, but it probably included only a few dozen men, both free citizens and servants.

Peter Minuit led the party of Swedish, Finnish, and Dutch colonists. Finland had long been a part of Sweden, but the Finns were seen as a different race from the Swedes. The Finns were disliked because they lived as migrants and practiced slash and burn agriculture. In other words, they moved across the countryside cutting and burning parts of the forest to make fields, and then moved on to repeat the process when the land wore out. It became a crime in Sweden to destroy woodland, and the crime was punishable by exile and servitude. So not everyone on the voyage was there by choice, nor could they all expect to grow wealthy from trade.

Peter Minuit was born in Germany to a French family, and worked for both the Dutch and the Swedish.

In addition to their provisions for the settlement, the colonists brought goods to trade with the native people for land and for furs. The New Sweden Company thought the Native Americans would most desire such items as axes, knives, pipes, mirrors, and cheap jewelry.

The expedition set sail in November 1637 and almost immediately received a battering from severe storms. The two ships became separated and had to return to port for repairs. They did not sail again until the end of December, and finally arrived at the Delaware River in March 1638.

After exploring the area and reassuring themselves that no other Europeans occupied the land, Minuit and his men chose a site on the western shore of the Delaware, on a creek running into the river, where modern Wilmington

Native peoples appreciated receiving metal cooking pots in exchange for furs

Right: The Swedes are often pictured making their land purchase on shore, but the sale was conducted aboard the *Kalmar Nyckel*. The Swedes believed they had purchased from the Indians all the land on the west bank of the Delaware River, extending from Cape Henlopen north to present-day Trenton, New Jersey, and reaching as far inland as they wished.

Below: An illustration from a Swedish book published in 1702 shows another artist's imaginary version of Swedes and Native Americans trading in New Sweden. The palm trees provide a clue that the artist had never seen New Sweden. Historians have discovered that the artist got his idea from a picture by another artist who also had never seen the Inative peoples of New Sweden.

stands today. Native Americans soon approached the settlers, and were invited aboard ship to sell some land. The amount of land the Native Americans thought they had sold differed greatly from the amount of land the Swedes believed they had bought, but that argument would not come up until later. Meanwhile, the Swedes built a fort and named it Fort Christina, after Sweden's young queen, and named the creek after her as well.

The first Swedes to sail to Delaware found a convenient rock ledge on which to land and unload their ships. The ledge, on the bank of Christina Creek, is today called Swede Rocks.

Inset: Voyagers crossing the Atlantic often encountered heavy storms.

3.
DELAWARE COUNTRY IN 1638

No part of present-day Delaware rises as high as 450 feet (137 meters) above sea level. Most of Delaware is coastal plain, bordered by Delaware Bay and Atlantic Ocean beaches, with only a small area of gently rolling hills known as the Piedmont, in the northwest corner. Many streams flow through Delaware into the Delaware River and Bay. Marshland surrounds much of the bay. Behind the marshes, the land was once heavily wooded, with mostly hardwood trees in the northern part of Delaware and mostly pines in the southern part.

About 12,000 Native Americans lived in small self-governing villages from the New Jersey seacoast to the Delaware Valley. They lived in large bark-covered buildings that each held up to 100 related people. They

A Delaware Native American village surrounded by a protective wall. Some Delaware villages were stockaded, while others were just houses built along riverbanks. These houses were built of birch poles covered with bark.

traveled around to hunt, fish, and gather wild plants. They also grew corn, beans, and squash. By 1700 barely 60 years later, fewer than 1,000 Native Americans lived in the same area. Many had died of European diseases such as smallpox. The rest moved westward, into the land that would soon be taken up by William Penn.

The Native Americans known to European colonists as the Delawares called themselves the Leni-Lenape. The first European to see Delaware, the English explorer Henry Hudson, sailed a Dutch ship into Delaware Bay in 1609. But it was the Virginia explorer, Samuel Argall, who sailed into Delaware Bay the following year and gave it an English name. Argall named it after Virginia's

Delaware had an abundance of trees, from which the colonists produced lumber for their own use and for trade.

Above: Sir Thomas West, Lord De la Warr, arrived to govern Virginia just as the colonists were about to give up and return to England. Virginia explorer Samuel Argall named Delaware Bay in his honor, though the governor never visited there.

colonial governor, Lord De la Warr. His name stuck, not only to the bay, but to a river, a colony, and an entire group of Native Americans.

Though Europeans saw the Delawares as one tribe, about ten distinct groups lived in independent villages around New Sweden. They all spoke an Algonquian language and lived in the northern part of Delaware at the time of first contact with Europeans. The Susquehannocks, who lived to the west of the Delawares, attacked them from time to time.

The Nanticokes in the southern and western parts of Delaware. They also spoke an Algonquian language and were closely related to the Delawares. Beginning in 1642, the Nanticokes fought with the Maryland colonists. This conflict greatly reduced the Nanticokes' numbers and eventually forced them to move north.

New Sweden, however, was not the first European colony in Delaware. A few years earlier in 1631, a Dutch merchant planted a fur-trading post in Delaware country,

near modern-day Lewes on the coast. They called it Swanendael, or valley of the swans. The following year, a neighboring Native American took a metal plate showing the Dutch coat of arms from a stake outside the post. Metal was almost unknown to the Native Americans, so the man probably just admired the object and wanted to show it to his people. The Dutch saw this as the theft of an important symbol of authority, and harshly protested to the chief. The chief, fearing the traders' anger, had the man executed. The dead man's supporters took revenge by ambushing and killing all of the Dutch settlers. No other European learned about the disaster until months later. The Dutch merchant returned to visit Swanendael and found it in ruins. He was able to learn the story from friendly Native Americans.

Opposite: One artist's idea of how the Leni Lenapes (Delawares) appeared during the days of New Sweden. Some European artists had difficulty drawing realistic pictures of Native Americans, and then later artists simply copied the earlier pictures. The Leni Lenapes traced their ancestry through their mothers. Delaware women could become engaged as soon as they were old enough to have children. They wore special headdresses to advertise their availability for marriage. Go-betweens arranged marriages; divorce was permitted if both husband and wife agreed.

Right: Early Delaware

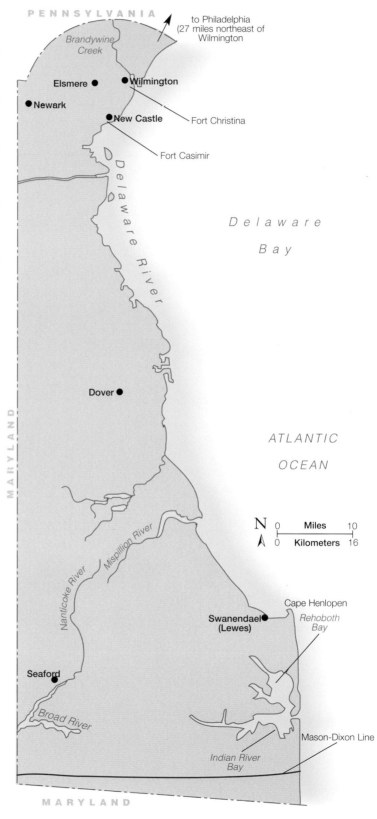

4.
NEW SWEDEN, 1638–1655

Peter Minuit left about 25 settlers at Fort Christina and began the return voyage to Europe aboard the *Kalmar Nyckel*, which the settlers had loaded with furs bought from the Native Americans. While docked at a Caribbean port, Minuit visited a nearby Dutch ship. A sudden storm came up, and the ship went down with Minuit on board. The *Kalmar Nyckel* returned home without him.

A Dutch officer in the Swedish navy, Peter Hollander Ridder, commanded the second voyage carrying more colonists to New Sweden in 1640. This voyage probably carried New Sweden's first women and children. The Dutch stockholders in the New Sweden Company invested in the second voyage, but they sold all their shares in 1641. Ridder remained as governor of the colony until 1643.

Unlike England, Sweden did not have a large population of discontented, unemployed laborers willing to try their luck across the ocean. Many of the New Sweden colonists had to be forced to leave Sweden. Army deserters and minor criminals were sentenced to exile and

Below: The first Swedish colonists arrive to claim New Sweden.

Above: This map of New Sweden appeared in a book published in Sweden in 1702. Unlike most maps, the south, and Delaware Bay, are at the top. In 1683, a Pennsylvania colonist described the Delaware River: "The River is a brave pleasant River as can be desired, affording divers[e] sorts of fish in great plenty, it's planted all along the Shore, and in some Creeks … mostly by Swedes, Finns, and Dutch, and now at last, English."

How to Build a Log Cabin

Sweden was a cold and heavily wooded land, and the Swedish knew how to build warm houses out of logs. In New Sweden, the Swedish settlers used the abundant trees they found to build the first log cabins of the colonies. Their method of notching logs at the corners to make them fit more closely was soon taken up by settlers all over the colonies. The English colonists in America came from a land with a milder climate than that of either America or Sweden, and they soon learned that log houses were warmer than their wood cottages. Before long, the log cabin became a familiar sight on frontier homesteads.

First, a settler had to cut down trees that were long and thick enough for a log cabin. It took about twenty logs per side to build a cabin. Each log was ten to twenty feet long and one to two feet in diameter. The size chosen depended on how many neighbors would be available to help move the logs and how long each wall of the cabin would be. Two workers using a crosscut saw cut the logs to the desired length.

Some builders chose to do the extra work of squaring off, or hewing, the sides of the logs with a broadaxe. The cabin builder used an axe, hatchet, or chisel to notch the ends of the logs so they could interlock. Swedes were especially skilled in the use of axe and wedge to cut trees and square logs, and many English neighbors learned the skill from them.

The entire cabin was usually built of one kind of log, preferably cedar or chestnut because they were water-resistant. Oak was too heavy and pine too flammable. Once they had prepared the logs, a family could put up a one-room cabin in three days, with the help of the other settlers. To keep out wind, rain, and pests, builders packed the spaces between the logs with mud and grass. They called this chinking the logs.

The openings for doors and windows had wooden frames attached to the logs with pegs. The door was made of wooden planks, and the roof of wooden shingles. Cabins often had no windows at all, or only one or two small openings covered by wooden shutters or animal skins. The earliest settlers did not have glass windows, and later frontier settlers could rarely afford glass. The fireplaces and chimneys were built either of stone, or of sticks and clay.

A close-up shows how logs for cabins are notched at the corners.

bundled aboard ships headed to America. More than two hundred years would pass before large numbers of Swedes, driven by poverty and overpopulation, would voluntarily come to America. Although the precise number is not known, probably no more than a thousand Swedes ever came to New Sweden, and the population barely reached 400 at its peak.

The small number of Swedish settlers had little choice but to get along with the Native Americans who lived around them. When the Delawares were attacked from the west by the Susquehannocks, who wanted to control all Native American trade with Europeans, the colonists were afraid to take sides. The Susquehannocks used guns they had acquired through trading with Europeans to drive the Delawares across the Delaware River into a small swampy area on its eastern bank in New Jersey. The defeated Delawares began moving farther north toward New Amsterdam. The Susquehannocks then turned south to fight the Maryland colonists in 1642.

Johan Printz, a Swedish army officer, arrived to serve as New Sweden's governor in 1643. His instructions from Queen Christina gave him absolute power over the colonists and the running of the colony. Printz governed New Sweden with an iron hand for ten years, and accomplished quite a lot considering how little he had to work with. Printz maintained friendly relations with the Native Americans, and convinced

Governor Johan Printz arrives at Fort Christina in 1643. His reports to the authorities in Sweden list the many difficulties the colony faced. "The reason that so many people died in the year 1643 was that they had then to begin to work, and but little to eat....The winter is sometimes so sharp, that I never felt it more severe in the northern parts of Sweden." Printz wrote again and again of the colony's lack of people to do the work: "The country is well suited for all sorts of cultivation; also for whale fishery and wine, if some one was here who understood the business." So many of the settlers had been transported to New Sweden by force that Printz reported, "All of them wish to be released, except the freemen."

ARRIVAL OF GOV. PRINTZ AT FORT CHRISTINA

the Dutch that New Sweden was not a threat to them. He also convinced a nearby group of English settlers either to leave the colony or swear allegiance to Sweden. The colony's modest but steady growth encouraged Printz to send settlers to occupy two new forts farther up the Delaware River. He moved the capital to Tinicum Island, in the Delaware River near the future site of Philadelphia, and called it New Gothenburg. He put the colonists to work building a couple of boats. Printz also ordered the colonists to concentrate on growing tobacco as a money-making crop.

Right: Fifty years old when he became governor of New Sweden, Johan Printz was said to weigh over 400 pounds. The Native Americans called him a name that translated to "Big Guts" or "Big Tub". He had been studying to become a Lutheran minister when he was forced to join the Swedish army. He turned out to be an excellent military officer.

Below: Governor Printz sent men out from the main fort to live in what he called strong houses, because they were solidly built and possible to defend.

In time, New Sweden began to suffer misfortunes. Crops did poorly and the colony had to purchase nearly all its food from its Native American, Dutch, and English neighbors. Settlers who had been forced to come to New Sweden did not work very hard, and Printz reported, "I

Governor Printz's plans for ship building faltered, as he reported in 1647: "… The hull is ready and floating on the water, but the completion of the work must be postponed until the arrival of a more skilled carpenter, the young men here declaring they do not know enough to finish it."

received … from the work of nine men hardly a year's nourishment for one man. Immediately I sent the sloop to [Manhattan] and caused to be bought there for the company seven oxen, one cow, and [75] bushels of winter rye." Printz's hopes of earning money from growing and

exporting tobacco came to little. The difficult work of clearing wooded land to create cropland went slowly. Tobacco, especially used up the soil's fertility, so that each crop was smaller than the one before.

A shipload of supplies and settlers from Sweden ran aground on a reef in the Caribbean in 1649, was captured by pirates, and never arrived. Then the young Queen Christina lost interest in New Sweden and sent no supplies or ships for four years. Trade with the Native Americans collapsed because New Sweden ran out of goods to trade. Colonists deserted or died, and the population fell to fewer than one hundred.

New Sweden was surrounded by jealous neighbors ready to take advantage of its diminishing strength. Both the Dutch in New Netherland and the English in Maryland believed they had a claim to Delaware. In 1651 New Netherland's governor, Peter Stuyvesant, sent 200 men to establish Fort Casimir, near present-day New Castle, only

Keeping the Peace

New Sweden survived as long as it did thanks to Governor Johan Printz s skill at negotiating with his neighbors. Printz kept himself well informed of the fights between Native Americans and colonists in the two neighboring colonies. In 1644 Printz reported back to Sweden on a massacre in Virginia, hundreds of Dutch losses in battles with the Native Americans, and raids in Maryland. Our [Native Americans] also become very [difficult] here in the river, Printz wrote of the Delawares. When some Delawares killed a couple in their home and two soldiers at New Sweden, Printz organized his men for defense. Seeing this, the Delawares came to apologize, swearing that they only wanted peace. Printz agreed, only on the condition that if the Delawares practiced the smallest hostilities against our people then we would not let a soul of them live. They sealed their agreement by signing a treaty and exchanging gifts. The Native Americans gave the Swedes some beaver pelts, and the Swedes gave the Native Americans a piece of cloth in return. But as Printz reported, They do not trust us and we trust them less.

While offering peace, Printz wrote to the New Sweden Company, Nothing would be better than that a couple of hundred soldiers should be sent here and kept here until we broke the necks of all of them in the river They are a lot of poor rascals. Then we could take possession of the places (which are the most fruitful) that the [Native Americans] now possess; then no one whether he be Hollander [Dutch] or Englishman could pretend in any manner to [claim] this place

The Dutch established Fort Casimir in 1651. When the Swedes captured it in 1654, they changed the name to Fort Trinity.

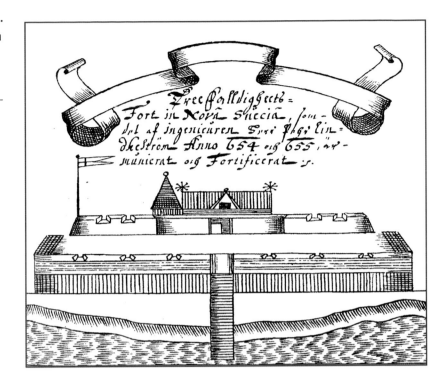

a few miles from Fort Christina. Stuyvesant's orders from home forbade him to directly attack New Sweden, because the Netherlands feared Sweden's mighty army. Governor Printz did not know what to do, but his letters to Queen Christina went unanswered. In 1653 Printz decided to return to Sweden and ask for help in person.

While Printz was sailing back to Sweden, the New Sweden Company's director convinced Queen Christina to send another expedition to her American colony. Several hundred settlers and their commander, Captain Johan Rising, set sail for Delaware. They arrived in May 1654. Finding Printz no longer there, Rising took over as governor.

Rising wasted no time in driving the Dutch from Fort Casimir. The careful diplomatic balancing act of Governor Printz was not for him. Rising wrote to Swedish authorities in June 1655, "The land is now practically clear of the Hollanders. It would be well if the same thing could be said of the English." Rising's action gave Peter Stuyvesant the excuse he needed to take over New Sweden. It could not be called an attack because Rising had struck first.

Stuyvesant's troops soon marched on New Sweden, retook Fort Casimir for New Netherland, and took control

When Dutch troops sailed up the Delaware and landed at Fort Trinity, Governor Rising knew he was out of reach of any help from home: "We had not sufficient strength for our defense, and were in want both of powder and other munitions, and had no hope of relief."

of the entire colony. New Sweden surrendered on September 15, 1655. While this was taking place, Native Americans had raided Dutch settlements along the Hudson River. This distracted Stuyvesant from New Sweden, so that he offered the Swedes generous terms. The Dutch allowed the Swedish settlers to either take their possessions and leave, or to swear loyalty to the Dutch and stay. Many stayed and were permitted to keep their property, and to keep attending their Lutheran churches. Few other colonies in America tolerated different religions.

5.
NEW NETHERLAND, SOUTH

Delaware now belonged to New Netherland, and Peter Stuyvesant was its governor. Between Stuyvesant's two colonies lay present-day New Jersey, then a trackless wilderness. New Amsterdam, the capital, and Delaware communicated by sea, sending ships from one to the other.

At first, the Dutch colonists who came to Delaware settled at New Amstel, in the country around Fort Casimir. Then they spread out to occupy more land.

The Dutch colonists brought African slaves with them to do some of the hard work of building a new colony. The

The Dutch community of New Amstel grew around Fort Casimir after New Sweden became part of New Netherland. After the English took over the colony, New Amstel became New Castle.

CONDITIEN,

Die door de Heeren BVRGERMEESTEREN *der Stadt Amstelredam*, volgens 't gemaeckte Accoordt met de *West-Indische Compagnie*, ende d'Approbatie van hare Hog. Mog. de Heeren STATEN GENERAEL *der Vereenighde Nederlanden*, daer op gevolght, gepresenteert werden aen alle de gene, die als Coloniers na Nieuw-Nederlandt willen vertrecken, &c.

t'AMSTERDAM,

By JAN BANNING, Ordinaris Drucker defer Stede, in 't jaer 1656.

In 1656, after capturing New Sweden, the Dutch advertised in Holland for more colonists.

new settlers drained some of Delaware's wetlands to create farms, just like the common practice in the Netherlands. They set up another settlement on the coast, near modern-day Lewes, in 1659, and started trading with the English colony of Maryland for tobacco, which they then shipped to Europe.

Like Sweden, England also had taken the Netherlands' side in the Thirty Years' War, but that war had ended in 1648. Soon, England and the Netherlands began to view one another as competitors for American trade goods. Their rivalry erupted into war on three separate occasions. During one of the wars, in 1664, a fleet of English ships

Cecilius Calvert (pictured), the second Lord Baltimore, lived until 1675. His son, Charles Calvert, served as governor of Maryland until his father died, and then became the third Lord Baltimore. Both men tried to claim Delaware as part of Maryland.

sailed into New Amsterdam's harbor and demanded Stuyvesant's surrender. The English fleet was too strong to resist, so Stuyvesant had to give in without a fight. New Netherland became New York, named for the king's brother, the Duke of York. The king gave the duke a land grant for New York, but the grant did not include Delaware. However, the king allowed the duke to govern Delaware along with New York.

The Lords Baltimore, who had established the privately owned Maryland colony, always believed that their charter also gave them control of the land around the Delaware Bay. So, they thought they should own

Delaware. In 1673 another war erupted between England and the Netherlands. A strong Dutch fleet sailed into New York harbor and forced the English governor to surrender without a fight. Lord Baltimore saw a chance to take over Delaware, since it was again held by an enemy of England. He sent a troop of horsemen to claim the land around Delaware Bay, supposedly for England, but really for himself. The horsemen fell upon the Dutch settlement near present-day Lewes on Christmas Eve, 1673. The Maryland troops burned the entire settlement, preventing the inhabitants—Dutch, Swedish, and English—from saving any of their possessions. The attackers took all boats, horses, guns, and food, and left the villagers stranded in the winter weather. The local Native Americans kindly took

....

Tobacco planters from Maryland moved to southern Delaware and built fine brick houses like the ones they had left behind. Growing tobacco drained the soil of its fertility, so planters hungered for new land.

The Swedish, Dutch, and English settlers of Delaware all grew tobacco or traded in it, so they could profit by selling it in Europe.

them in until the Dutch authorities sent aid. One survivor reported, "The **Indians** [Native Americans] that lived here about wept when they saw the spoil that the inhabitants had suffered by their own native countrymen."

A year later, the Dutch and the English signed a treaty that returned the Netherlands' North American possessions to England for good. Lord Baltimore was not permitted to keep Delaware. Although physically isolated from New York, Delaware resumed its status as a part of New York. Gradually, English people from New York and Maryland moved to Delaware and took up farming. The Marylanders preferred the southern part of Delaware, which most closely resembled Maryland. They came with their slaves and built tobacco plantations. Still, life in Delaware remained much the same as it had been when the population was mostly Swedish and Dutch. The colonial government encouraged people to settle the area by offering land grants of 50 acres per person.

Since New York was far away, New Castle, once called New Amstel by the Dutch, served as an unofficial capital for Delaware, and Delaware was divided into three counties. The colonial governor of New York approved a set of English laws of governing the outlying parts of the colony. However, ten years went by before anyone sent a copy of the laws to Delaware.

INDIANS: NAME GIVEN TO ALL NATIVE AMERICANS AT THE TIME EUROPEANS FIRST CAME TO AMERICA, BECAUSE IT WAS BELIEVED THAT AMERICA WAS ACTUALLY A CLOSE NEIGHBOR OF INDIA

Right "Mighty Whales roll upon the Coast, near the Mouth of the Bay of Delaware … We justly hope a considerable profit by a Whalery; they being so numerous …" wrote William Penn in 1685.

Below: In 1660 Charles II was restored to the throne of England. He had been living in exile in Europe, having fled for his life when his father, Charles I, was executed during the English Civil War.

6.
PENN'S WOODS, EAST

Events in England had a great influence on the distribution of land for colonies. In 1660, when King Charles II regained the throne of England, he received help and money from his good friend, Admiral Sir William Penn. The king was never able to pay him back, but instead, in 1681, gave Penn's son, William Penn, a large piece of land for a colony in America.

William Penn was concerned that his colony,

William Penn, was proprietor (owner) of Delaware.

Pennsylvania (Penn's Woods), did not have direct access to the sea. So the king's brother, the Duke of York, also grateful to Admiral Penn for his help, gave William Penn the three counties of Delaware in 1682, though the duke did not formally own them.

During their association with Pennsylvania, the three counties on the lower Delaware River were actually called the "Counties of New Castle, Kent, and Sussex on the Delaware," or simply, "the Lower Counties." Almost a century passed before the counties officially united under the name Delaware.

William Penn instructed the three lower counties to elect **delegates** to the **assembly** of Pennsylvania. This marked the first time that Delaware had a true representative government. The assembly formalized the

DELEGATE: PERSON ELECTED TO REPRESENT THE VOTERS' INTERESTS IN THE LEGISLATURE

ANGLICAN: BELONGING TO THE CHURCH OF ENGLAND, A PROTESTANT CHURCH AND THE STATE CHURCH OF ENGLAND

union between the Pennsylvania and Delaware counties, and adopted the constitution proposed by Penn.

Lord Baltimore tried once again to claim Delaware for Maryland. He thought that William Penn would be easier to defeat than the king's brother. Also, Penn was a **Quaker,** and Quakers were unpopular both in England and in the colonies. But the royal family's loyalty to the Penn family remained true. When the Duke of York became King James II in 1685, he made up a deed to give Penn formal ownership of Delaware. But in 1688 he was forced from the throne and had to flee England before he could make the deed official. The Penn family and the Lords

Above: King Charles II's brother was the Duke of York. When the royal family returned to England in 1660, Admiral Penn (William's father) and the duke together ran England's navy department. When the English drove the Dutch from America, the king gave New Netherland to the Duke of York, and so it became New York. When Charles II died in 1685, his brother became King James II.

QUAKER: ORIGINALLY A TERM OF MOCKERY GIVEN TO MEMBERS OF THE SOCIETY OF FRIENDS, A CHRISTIAN GROUP FOUNDED IN ENGLAND AROUND 1650

Sweden first sent a Lutheran minister to New Sweden in 1640. Lutheran ministers continued to emigrate to Delaware, to serve the Swedish and Finnish Lutherans, until the Revolution. Ericus Bjork, a Lutheran minister, sailed from Sweden to Delaware in 1697 to serve the Lutherans of the Wilmington area.

BRITISH: NATIONALITY OF A PERSON BORN IN GREAT BRITAIN; PEOPLE BORN IN ENGLAND ARE CALLED "ENGLISH"

ANGLICAN: BELONGING TO THE CHURCH OF ENGLAND, A PROTESTANT CHURCH AND THE STATE CHURCH OF ENGLAND

PACIFIST: PERSON AGAINST WAR AND VIOLENCE; THE BELIEFS OF SUCH A PERSON

Opposite: Swedish Lutherans remained free to practice their religion after the fall of New Sweden. Crane Hook church was built in the style of a simple Swedish log cabin in 1667, to replace the original church at Fort Christina. The New Sweden colonists were America's first Lutherans. Lutherans were Protestants, followers of the German monk, Martin Luther, who protested against the Roman Catholic church in 1517.

Baltimore became involved in a long lawsuit over ownership of Delaware, and more than 70 years would pass before the **British** court settled the suit in the Penns' favor, in 1750. In the meantime, Delaware remained under the ownership of the crown, who permitted it to be governed as part of Pennsylvania.

The residents of Delaware resented their counties being acquired by Penn. Most were **Anglicans** or Lutherans, and they disliked Quakers. Quakers held a majority in the Pennsylvania assembly. Because of the Quakers' **pacifist** (antiwar) beliefs, they refused to vote funding for military defense of the Delaware Valley. Delaware residents living near the coast feared attacks by

Some of the Scotch-Irish were well educated and found work as school teachers or private tutors for the children of wealthy families.

pirates, and with good reason. Pennsylvania's assemblymen could afford to ignore the matter of defense because Delaware served as a buffer against attack by sea.

William Penn had returned to England in 1684 to pursue his claim to Delaware. The overthrow of James II, however, led to Penn being jailed and his colony being placed under royal control for several years. But Penn's friends defended him, and his colony was returned to his control. When Penn finally returned to America in 1699, he found that the representatives of the Pennsylvania and Delaware counties could not cooperate. Fearing that he would lose the Delaware counties entirely, in 1702 William Penn permitted their delegates to meet separately from those of Pennsylvania. The Pennsylvanians were happy to see this separation take place, because they resented having to share power with the Delaware

INDENTURED SERVANT:
PERSON WHO AGREED TO
WORK AS A SERVANT FOR A
CERTAIN NUMBER OF YEARS
IN EXCHANGE FOR FOOD,
CLOTHING, A PLACE TO
SLEEP, AND PAYMENT OF
ONE'S PASSAGE ACROSS THE
ATLANTIC TO THE
COLONIES

SCOTCH-IRISH: SCOTTISH
PEOPLE WHO SETTLED IN
NORTHERN IRELAND
DURING THE EARLY 1600S.
MANY WERE DRIVEN BY
POVERTY TO EMIGRATE TO
AMERICA AS INDENTURED
SERVANTS.

counties. The English government never formally recognized the separation, but it occurred nevertheless. The separate Delaware assembly first met in New Castle in 1704. Their laws still had to be approved by Pennsylvania's governor, and the governor also appointed Delaware's judges and other legal officials.

The 1700s saw migration into Delaware from several places. Slave-owning English tobacco **planters** left Maryland and Virginia, where they had used up the soil's fertility, and set up plantations in southern Delaware. Delaware tried to pass a law forbidding the importation of slaves, but the Pennsylvania governor vetoed it.

After about 1715, several thousand **Scotch-Irish** came to Delaware, often as **indentured servants**. As Presbyterians, many chose Delaware because it was one of only three colonies that did not have an established church (the other two were Pennsylvania and Rhode Island). More than a thousand Quakers moved from Pennsylvania to Delaware during the 1700s. Both groups settled in the area around New Castle, in the northern part of Delaware. Wilmington, too, began to grow as a city in the mid-1700s.

Right: New Castle in 1750 was a growing town under British rule.

As tobacco gradually wore out the soil, wheat and corn became Delaware's major crops. Large mills along such creeks as the Brandywine turned out flour and meal, much of which was shipped to Philadelphia and exported. Peach orchards thrived in Delaware since the colony's earliest days. The farms along the Delaware River and other waterways benefited from their ability to easily transport their produce by boat. Delaware also exported lumber from its abundant woodlands.

Delaware endured several costly and destructive attacks from the sea. In 1698 pirates looted the coastal settlement of Lewes. Lewes was again looted by French

Below: A drawing shows a farm outside of Wilmington.

Below: This New Castle home was built around 1730.

sailors in 1709, and in 1747, two plantations on Delaware Bay were attacked by foreign ships. After Delaware gained a separate **legislature**, the colony issued paper **currency** to pay for its own defense.

Delaware also raised militia to assist **Great Britain** in fighting battles in its other colonies. Delaware militia went to New England in 1746 to help fight King George's War, which Great Britain fought to try to expel France from Canada.

In 1754 war again broke out between Great Britain and France. The two nations fought for control of territories in North America, the West Indies, Europe, and India. In America, they fought for control of the land west of the Allegheny Mountains, and the war came to be called the French and Indian War. In Europe the war was called the Seven Years' War. Delaware militia again helped Great Britain during the French and Indian War. In 1758 Delaware troops worked on building a road to Fort Duquesne, in western Pennsylvania, so the British could capture it. Great

LEGISLATURE: GROUP OF REPRESENTATIVES ELECTED TO MAKE LAWS

CURRENCY: COINS OR PAPER USED AS MONEY

GREAT BRITAIN: NATION FORMED BY ENGLAND, WALES, SCOTLAND, AND NORTHERN IRELAND; "GREAT BRITAIN" CAME INTO USE WHEN ENGLAND AND SCOTLAND FORMALLY UNIFIED IN 1707

Population Growth, 1650–1770

In 1650 New Sweden held about 185 men, women, and children. Fifteen of them were African slaves. After the Dutch takeover, the population grew to about 500 European settlers and 30 African slaves.

The colony's years as an outpost of New York saw the population, both white and African, double. After Pennsylvania took over the three Delaware counties, the European population grew faster. By 1700 the white population was 2,500, the African, 135.

By 1770 both the white population of Delaware and the number of slaves had grown dramatically. Delaware had more than 35,000 people, of whom about 7,000 were black, most of them slaves. Although slavery did not end in Delaware until 1865, many of Delaware's people were influenced by the growing antislavery movement and freed their slaves during and after the Revolution. By 1790 nearly one in three of Delaware's blacks were free.

Delaware's population at the time of the Revolution was about 50% English, 20% black, 10% Irish, 8% Scottish, 7% Swedish, 4% Dutch, and 1% German.

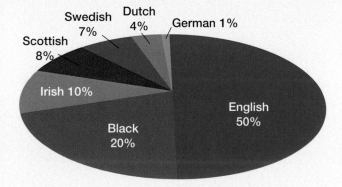

Swedish 7%
Dutch 4%
German 1%
Scottish 8%
Irish 10%
English 50%
Black 20%

Britain's victory in the French and Indian War gave Canada to the British in 1763, but it did not put an end to Native American raids on the western frontier. Native Americans had been pushed westward, out of Delaware and all the way through Pennsylvania, and they wanted revenge.

Above: Seaside colonial plantations such as this one had beautiful ocean views but faced the danger of attacks by pirates.

Displaced Delaware Native Americans joined the Shawnees in a rebellion in 1763. They raided frontier homes and took settlers captive, forcing the British to bargain for their release.

7.
MOVING NATIVE AMERICANS WEST

Throughout the history of European settlement in Delaware, relations between Native Americans and settlers were usually peaceful, marked by only a few minor raids by Native Americans on isolated settlers.

By the time William Penn founded his colony along the western side of the Delaware River, the population of the Delaware people had been sharply reduced by disease. The small remaining population, without protest, sold much of their land along the Delaware River to William Penn's

A village of Delaware Native Americans migrates westward.

colony. However, so vaguely did the deeds state the boundaries of the purchased land that arguments later broke out between the Delawares and William Penn's descendants.

As settlers built fences and prevented the Delawares from hunting, most of the Native Americans moved north and west, beyond the line of colonial settlement. Those that stayed behind had to get British approval whenever a new chief took power. The British colonists met with the Delawares several times between 1756 and 1758 and set up a reservation for them in New Jersey. Over time, however, most Delawares left the area and moved westward.

Farther south in Delaware colony, the Nanticokes who had once lived there now held only a handful of small

reservations. Even the reservations suffered from English encroachments, and the remaining Nanticokes moved to Pennsylvania during the 1700s. By the 1750s, many Nanticokes and Delawares were living far beyond Pennsylvania, in the Ohio River valley.

The Native Americans who migrated west to Ohio were the ones who most wanted to resist the British and maintain their traditional way of life. Many of the Delawares who relocated to the Ohio Valley joined with the Shawnees during the mid-1700s. The outbreak of the French and Indian War, and Great Britain's first major defeat in western Pennsylvania in 1755, encouraged the Shawnees and Delawares to cross Pennsylvania and raid settlements in the Delaware Valley.

Delaware raiders picked off settlers family by family, but Delaware colonists did not suffer large-scale massacres like those that occurred in Virginia.

Above: English surveyors at work

Delaware's Changing Borders

Delaware is bordered by the Delaware Bay, Pennsylvania, and Maryland. Its longest border is with Maryland. As an unofficial part of Pennsylvania, Delaware suffered through that colony s border dispute with Maryland. Colonists unfortunate enough to live near the Delaware-Maryland border faced the possibility of arrest by either colony for nonpayment of taxes.

After the British courts awarded Delaware to the Penn family in 1750, American surveyors started working on the border. But the descendants of Penn and Lord Baltimore decided to hire the English surveyors Charles Mason and Jeremiah Dixon to finish the complicated job. The two men began work in 1763 and finished in 1767. Their survey created the Mason-Dixon Line, which consists of both the Maryland-Pennsylvania and the Maryland-Delaware borders. Mason and Dixon finished marking the Delaware part of the border in 1765. The Mason-Dixon survey gave Delaware additional territory in both the western and southern parts of the colony and added former Maryland citizens to Delaware s population.

The Mason-Dixon Line began as the solution to a persistent colonial border dispute. It later became an important symbol to Americans, of the division between the North and the South during the Civil War.

Below: Depending on who drew the map, Cape Henlopen, on the Delaware Bay, lay in either Maryland or Delaware. In the end it belonged to Delaware.

8.
REBELLION

The French and Indian War had been expensive for Great Britain, so the British Parliament imposed new taxes on the colonies to help pay for the war. The first major new tax law was the Sugar Act of 1764. The act called for import and export duties, or taxes, to be paid on many trade goods, such as sugar, coffee, indigo, and

Nearby Philadelphia, the biggest city in Pennsylvania, and in the British colonies, had a great influence on life in Delaware. It was the market to which Delaware sent most of its products, the place where the governor made his decisions, and a center of education and culture.

Thomas McKean was a signer of the Declaration of Independence.

animal hides. The British sent ships to patrol the American coast and enforce the law. They also assigned customs officials to collect the **taxes** and had merchants arrested who were thought to be evading the taxes. Next, in 1765 **Parliament** passed the Stamp Act. Under the Stamp Act, colonists had to pay to have most documents stamped, or risk arrest. Even newspapers had to have stamps. The Stamp Act affected colonists of all social classes, and resistance grew throughout the colonies.

Delaware was a small colony that was influenced by the larger colonies around it. Many of its citizens had moved there from neighboring colonies. Nearby Philadelphia had the greatest influence on Delaware. Delaware citizens read Philadelphia newspapers and sent their sons to school there. So when Philadelphians objected to British taxes, the protests quickly spread to Delaware. Delaware's Scotch-Irish immigrants especially objected to the new laws because they already disliked

Born in Maryland in 1733, George Read was the son of prosperous Irish immigrants and attended school in Pennsylvania. He studied law under a Philadelphia lawyer. Pennsylvania's governor appointed him attorney general of the Delaware counties. In 1765 Read was elected to Delaware's assembly, and in 1776 he was elected president of Delaware's constitutional convention.

the English and blamed them for the hardships they had suffered in Ireland.

When the colonies held the 1765 Stamp Act Congress in New York to protest the taxes, Delaware sent two delegates, Caesar Rodney, a wealthy landowner, and Thomas McKean, a lawyer. Parliament repealed the Stamp Act in 1766, but soon passed additional taxes. The colonies then formed Committees of Correspondence that communicated by writing letters. The Committees kept **patriots** in the colonies informed and made plans to cooperate in a **boycott** of British goods.

Word got out that some Delaware merchants were trying to get around the boycott and import British merchandise through Maryland. Community leaders met and created committees of inspection to enforce the boycott in each town. George Read, a New Castle lawyer and a delegate to the Delaware assembly, supervised the committees. The boycott convinced the British to repeal most taxes by 1770, except for the tax on tea.

PATRIOTS: AMERICANS WHO WANTED THE COLONIES TO BE INDEPENDENT OF GREAT BRITAIN

BOYCOTT: an agreement to refuse to buy from or sell to certain businesses or people

Opposite, Top: Colonists enjoyed the "sport" of cockfighting, in which specially bred roosters fought to the death while spectators bet on which would win. Fans of the sport believed that roosters hatched by a type of chicken called "blue hen" made especially fierce fighters.

Relieved of tax burdens for a while, the colonies prospered, and colonial life remained calm until 1773. Few colonists really wanted independence from Great Britain as long as they could make their own laws and set their own taxes. Then Parliament passed a law that gave one British tea seller, the East India Company, special treatment. The East India Company was given a monopoly in the colonies so that it could sell its tea more cheaply than any other dealer. Once again, the Committees of Correspondence went to work, spreading news of the new law and the coming East India Company tea shipments and organizing actions against the shipments.

The first action, the famous Boston Tea Party, occurred in December 1773 with the dumping of a large tea shipment into Boston Harbor. Great Britain responded to the Boston Tea Party by closing the port of Boston and placing Massachusetts under military rule. Delaware's Committee of Correspondence called mass meetings in each of the three counties. The people voted to support Massachusetts and to send delegates to a

Right: Because of his epic night ride, Caesar Rodney is as famous in Delaware as Paul Revere is in Massachusetts.

Opposite, Bottom: The 1st Delaware regiment, one of the finest in George Washington's army, called themselves the "Blue Hen's Chickens," after Delaware's famous fighting roosters. Colonel John Haslet, a Scotch-Irish immigrant, organized the regiment in 1776.

Continental Congress to be held in Philadelphia in September 1774. Delaware sent three delegates to the Continental Congress: Thomas McKean, George Read, and Caesar Rodney.

The congress drew up a set of resolutions stating the rights of the colonies to self-government. They also formed a Continental Association to boycott British trade goods and organize local governments. Finally, the Congress agreed to meet again in May 1775. Before that date arrived, the first battle of the American Revolution had been fought in Massachusetts.

After the meeting of the Second Continental Congress, which created the Continental Army, Delaware set up new committees to enforce the boycott and to recruit, arm, and train soldiers for the coming Revolution. The First Delaware Regiment would earn a reputation as one of the Continental Army's best units.

On June 15, 1776, the Delaware assembly voted to

In a clever political move, the Continental Congress waited an extra day to count the votes, and thus made sure that the Declaration of Independence received unanimous approval.

suspend all British royal authority in Delaware. This vote effectively declared Delaware's independence from the government of Pennsylvania as well. Only two weeks later, the Continental Congress began to debate whether the colonies should declare their independence from Great Britain. Read, Rodney, and McKean were again the delegates from Delaware. Rodney was absent from the debate because he was general of a **militia,** and his troops had been called to put down a small **loyalist** rebellion in Sussex County. McKean voted for independence and Read voted against it. Learning of the tie between the two men, Caesar Rodney made a historic overnight ride to Philadelphia, arriving on July 2, 1776. He voted for independence, so that Delaware had to cast its one vote for independence. All three Delaware delegates then signed the Declaration of Independence.

The following month, the three Delaware counties renamed themselves the Delaware State and held a convention to write a state constitution and organize a state government. The state constitution prohibited the slave trade and guaranteed freedom of the press and freedom of religion (for Christians only). To be permitted to vote, men had to own at least 50 acres of land or a valuable business.

During the Revolution, British troops marched through Delaware, and British ships sailed up the Delaware River. For safety, Delaware's capital was moved from New Castle to Dover in 1777.

British ships fight their way past Delaware River forts during the Revolution.

EPILOGUE

After the Revolution, Delaware became the first state to ratify the United States Constitution on December 7, 1787. Delaware is the second smallest state in the United States, larger only than Rhode Island. It is 35 miles (56 kilometers) wide at its widest point. Delaware and New Jersey disputed ownership of the Delaware River where it forms the boundary between the two states, until the U.S. Supreme Court decided in 1935 that most of the river lies in Delaware.

About 750,000 people live in modern Delaware. About 80% of them are of European descent. A few hundred Nanticoke Native Americans live in southwestern Delaware. Although Delaware outlawed the importation of slaves in 1776, slavery itself remained legal in the state until the end of the Civil War.

Delaware still has abundant wildlife, such as deer, foxes, raccoons, opossum, muskrats, and waterfowl. Yet some of its natural resources have suffered. During the late 1800s, a virus destroyed most of the state's peach orchards. A parasite has nearly destroyed the oyster population of Delaware Bay. However, Delaware Bay

Muskrats have always thrived on Delaware's many waterways.

A view along the Delaware River

Right: The Du Pont Company powder mills near Wilmington in 1882. The company was a major supplier of gunpowder to the Union Army.

Below: The Old Swedes Church in Wilmington was built in 1698. It is one of the oldest standing churches in the United States. It started as a Swedish Lutheran church, then became Anglican, and is now Episcopalian.

crabs, however, are widely sold. Delaware's ocean beaches attract a great many tourists.

The chemical industry, which had its start in 1802 with the DuPont powder mill, is Delaware's major modern industry. Delaware is also a center for banking. Sussex County is still agricultural and has many poultry farms.

Two buildings from the colonial era can still be visited: the Old Dutch House in New Castle, and the Old Swedes Church in Wilmington.

The Old Dutch House, built in New Castle during the late 1600s, is probably the oldest house still standing in Delaware.

MANHATTAN PURCHASE: Dutch purchase of Manhattan Island, the center of present-day New York City, in 1626 from the local Native Americans for about $24 worth of trinkets and cheap jewelry.

MERCHANT: trader; person who buys and re-sells merchandise

MILITIA: group of citizens not normally part of the army who join together to defend their land in an emergency

NATIVE AMERICANS: people who had been living in America for thousands of years at the time that the first Europeans arrived

NETHERLANDS: European nation formed by the union of several low-lying provinces, including Holland. Amsterdam is the capital. People there are known as "Dutch."

NEW WORLD: western hemisphere of the earth, including North America, Central America, and South America; so called because the people of the Old World, in the east, did not know about the existence of the Americas until the 1400s

OUTPOST: fort or settlement located far from the main settlement

PACIFIST: person against war and violence; the beliefs of such a person

PARLIAMENT: legislature of Great Britain

PATRIOTS: Americans who wanted the colonies to be independent of Great Britain

PLANTER: owner of a plantation, or large farm

QUAKER: originally a term of mockery given to members of the Society of Friends, a Christian group founded in England around 1650

SCOTCH-IRISH: Scottish people who settled in northern Ireland during the early 1600s. Many were driven by poverty to emigrate to America as indentured servants.

SURVEY: map showing the boundaries of a parcel of land, drawn as a record of land ownership

TAX: payment required by the government

THIRTY YEARS' WAR: war fought throughout Europe from 1618 to 1648. The war began as a religious war between Roman Catholics and Protestants for control of Germany, but other nations joined the fighting. Enormous destruction of lives and property occurred across Europe.

VIKINGS: Scandinavian people who traveled in long, oared boats to raid coastal and some inland settlements of Europe during the 8th, 9th, and 10th centuries

FURTHER READING

Smith, Carter, ed. *Battles in a New Land: A Source Book on Colonial America.* Brookfield, Conn.: Millbrook Press, 1991.

Smith, Carter, ed. *Explorers and Settlers: A Source Book on Colonial America.* Brookfield, Conn.: Millbrook Press, 1991.

Tunis, Edwin. *Colonial Living.* Baltimore: Johns Hopkins University Press, 1999.

WEBSITES

http://americanhistory.si.edu/hohr/springer
Study objects and documents to piece together the life of a New Castle, Delaware, family in the 1700s.

www.americaslibrary.gov
Select "Jump back in time" for links to history activities.

http://www.delawaretribeofindians.nsn.us/
Explore this site run by the Delaware Indians, containing information about the tribe for Indians and non-Indians

Disclaimer
All Internet addresses (URLs) given in this book were valid at the time it went to press. However, due to the dynamic nature of the Internet, some addresses may have changed, or sites may have ceased to exist since publication. While the author and publisher regret any inconvenience this may cause readers, no responsibility for any such changes can be accepted by either the author or the publisher.

BIBLIOGRAPHY

Middleton, Richard. *Colonial America: A History, 1607–1760.* Cambridge, Mass.: Blackwell, 1992.

Munroe, John A. *History of Delaware.* Newark, Del.: University of Delaware, 2001.

Myers, Albert Cook. *Narratives of Early Pennsylvania, West New Jersey, and Delaware: 1630–1707.* New York: Charles Scribner's Sons, 1912.

Taylor, Alan. *American Colonies.* New York: Viking, 2001.

The American Heritage History of the Thirteen Colonies. New York: American Heritage Publishing, 1967.

INDEX